QUIT YOUR JOB OFTEN AND GET BIG RAISES!

QUIT YOUR JOB OFTEN AND GET BIG RAISES!

A REAL-WORLD PRACTICAL GUIDE TO
DRAMATICALLY INCREASE YOUR WAGES, AS TOLD BY
AN AVERAGE WORKING STIFF WHO QUIT FOUR JOBS
IN FIVE YEARS AND TRIPLED HIS PAY!

GORDON MILLER

MAIN STREET BOOKS

DOUBLEDAY

New York   London   Toronto   Sydney   Auckland

A Main Street Book
PUBLISHED BY DOUBLEDAY

a division of Bantam Doubleday Dell Publishing Group, Inc.
1540 Broadway, New York, New York, 10036

Main Street Books, Doubleday, and the portrayal of a building with a
tree are trademarks of Doubleday, a division of Bantam Doubleday Dell
Publishing Group, Inc.

Book design by Stanley S. Drate/Folio Graphics Co. Inc.

Library of Congress Cataloging-in-Publication Data

Miller, Gordon, 1948–
Quite your job often and get big raises!: a real world practical
guide to dramatically increase your wages, as told by an average
working stiff who quit 4 jobs in 5 years and tripled his pay!/
Gordon Miller.—1st Main Street Books ed.
p.   cm.
1. Career development.   2. Promotions.   3. Career changes
I. Title.
HF5381.M486   1998   IN PROCESS
650.14—dc21   98-40686
CIP

To my darling Deborah (the Dream goes on). You are incredible. Brett, Kacey (Brandon, Ryan). I adore you. Family and Friends. Thanks for being there (and putting up with me).

CONTENTS

Quit Your Job Often
and Get Big Raises!

PROLOGUE

So you're tired of getting 3 or 4 percent annual raises? Or no raises at all while corporate profits are going through the roof? (You may not be aware of it, but Real Corporate Profits have increased more than 50 percent in the last five years while Real Median Wages have decreased during the same period. Just thought you'd like to know.) The words *merger, acquisition, downsizing, rightsizing* and *re-engineering* have taken on new meaning. You suddenly realize that Dilbert may know a lot more about your work situation than your manager does.

If any or all of those statements ring true, this small volume may be the most important book you read this year. Or any year.

What you will read is a true story. I know that because I lived it. The information didn't come to me on stone tablets or in a dream from some figure clothed in white light. I take a solemn oath that I am not now, nor have I ever been, a guru of any kind. Like most of the things I've learned, it's been trial and error, usually more error than trial.

I don't have an M.B.A. from Harvard or Stanford. In fact, I'm not a scholar of any kind. I'm a small-town guy from Iowa raised with traditional values and a strong work ethic. My father worked for one company for forty years, retired, lived poor and died broke. I was raised to believe that the old values still worked. The truth is—they don't always. Not in today's world. One of the first things you need to understand is that . . .

THE RULES HAVE CHANGED

. . . and unless you're willing and able to adapt, you'll surely go the way of the saber-toothed tiger.

Ten years ago I was making $40,000 a year, plugging along, thinking that if I was loyal, trustworthy, brave and true, the company would compensate me appropriately. Soon enough it became clear that they wouldn't, and though they still believed in the concept of loyalty, they would much rather have it be my loyalty than theirs. Today, a short ten years later, I am making approximately four times that much.

How did I do it? Well, that's what this book

is about. It is, above all, a practical guide (we'll leave the theory to the Harvard and Stanford guys), a step-by-step process of learning how to make the New Rules work in your favor. There will be research for you to do, actions for you to take. I am not about to suggest that you stand on the street corner with a WILL WORK FOR STOCK OPTIONS sign. There is risk involved. This book will help you minimize that risk.

The time is right. It has never been better.

1

THE RULES HAVE CHANGED

or

*How to Make Lemonade When
They Hand You Lemons*

*O*n July 13, 1997, two days after I quit my fourth job in five years, the most interesting thing happened. I got three job offers and a 30 percent pay increase.

Why, you ask?

Simple . . . The Rules Have Changed.

There are several reasons for the changes: the globalization of the economy (over 50 percent of Hewlett-Packard's income is now derived from overseas markets—and they are only one of many), mergers and acquisitions, new advances in technology and the concept of *outsourcing* noncore functions. The entire business economy has changed. The old ways may no longer be effective. Companies are changing strategies in order to stay competitive. They are realizing that they must not only be willing to change but be willing to change quickly in response to new technologies, to new business and manufacturing demands. At one time business drove the market; today it's the other way around. Twenty-five years ago it was a different story.

In the fifties and sixties, long-term manufacturing and business planning was a viable activity. And in those days *long-term* meant years. (I mean, how much difference was there between a 1951 and a 1961 toaster?) Now, *long-term* is more likely measured in months, sometimes weeks. Technology dictates a fundamental change in attitude and outlook. The feeling that everything is going a lot faster is not an illusion.

To Market, to Market, to Market We Go . . .

And you'd better hurry, because if you don't . . . Well, need we say more? The corporate landscape is littered with the abandoned dreams of businesses that were not in a position to be flexible and responsive. Workers, too. Faster than anyone could have imagined, 286's became 386's, which became 486's, which seemingly overnight turned into Pentiums and Workstations and Lans and Wans and God knows what else. What's next? State-of-the-art is what's in the morning mail. And that's each morning's mail. As in e-mail.

The Old Model says that Workers are faithful, loyal, trustworthy and true; they toil long and hard and get small annual raises, work at least five years before a Promotion comes along, at least another five before an actual Position is available. From there, it's ten years' minimum to a Desk and a tie and a small plastic placard with your name on it. GORDON MILLER. You've arrived. At last. But if the process was slow, at least it was usually reliable. Usually . . . Your loyalty was to some extent returned. (That was in the days before the Merger and Acquisition Monster was born. Such a cute baby. How could we have known?) Of course, as you know by now, that kind of loyalty is a thing of the past. It is dead. D-e-a-d. Why? Because it's no longer good business. Companies have to change quickly or they won't be in business very long . . . *Goodbye, Mr. and Mrs. Worker. You're not the Mr. and Mrs. Worker we need for this project. See ya . . .*

Oh, companies still talk about loyalty. They have Human Resources Departments, Employee Assistance Programs, and they will tell you that loyalty is important, but the truth is you'll be down-sized right out the door so fast you'll get a nosebleed when and if the company decides that you no longer fit into their plans. The paradigm (now there's a nice Harvard word) has changed. Congratulations, you're now a casualty of re-engineering. No Purple Heart—just a plain old Pink Slip.

Some twenty years ago yours truly entered the Wonderful World of Business. Remember now, I'm just your basic, no-frills, small-town Iowa guy with the olde tyme work ethic. Some schooling. Nothing special. But eager. And do I ever want to make good. Wanna be a Team Player . . . *Nose to the grindstone. Idleness is the devil's workshop. A penny saved is a penny earned* . . . You know. Stuff I learned from my father, the guy who put a lot into a system that he believed in, lived poor in retirement and died broke. The irony of it is that he still believed in the system when he died. How's that for brainwashing?

The horror stories are almost endless. Nearly everyone of my father's generation has one to tell. First, the Medical Retiree Plan somehow disappears. Poof, like magic. Medicare won't cover all the prescriptions, and then there is Alzheimer's . . . *Too expensive, and you old guys are sick too often . . . I know we promised, but we can't do it anymore. So sue me* . . . Then perhaps the Acquisition and Merger Monster strikes and the Pension Plan, your carefully nurtured nest egg for the Golden Years (remember those?), also does an el foldo and you have Lost Out. You are now a statistic. A thorough investigation is under way. Indictments may be handed down at any moment . . . *In the meantime, we're sorry to inform you that . . . you're . . . screwed . . .* Do we suspect foul play here, Watson? We certainly do, but there's nothing we can do about it.

So those of us who are relying on the old conventions to pull us through are in for some surprises. There's no place to run and no place to hide in the present business climate. Time to face the music: Old strategies may not work. Old career paths may not be successful. It's good business for companies to get you to be loyal, though it may not be such good business for you personally. Ask any of the 70,000 men and women at IBM who lost their jobs in the nineties. Loyal to Big Blue? Sure were. How about the thousands of folks at AT&T who were laid off? And just to rub a little salt in the wounds, a recent CEO at AT&T was cashiered after less than a year on the job and received one of those Golden Parachutes to the tune of $30,000,000! That's thirty million for those of us who are confused by all the zeroes.

Might have been able to salvage a few jobs at that price. But since the people voting on the severance package are other managers hoping for similar treatment, it's expected that the coffers will be opened for one of their fallen comrades.

And to put it in very recent terms, here's an account of some notable job layoff announcements during 1998:

Amoco	6,000
Boeing	28,000
Compaq	17,000
Intel	3,000
Motorola	15,000
Fruit of the Loom	5,000

(So who needs all that underwear anyway?)

And who benefits from loyalty if it's a one-way street? You're absolutely right—the Company. See? You're already beginning to learn. (I knew you were smart when you bought the book.) The Company mantra is *Be grateful, be grateful. After all, you do have a job. You know how many people don't? Have jobs? Thousands, pal. Maybe millions. Think about it.*

A good friend of mine worked for a large software company for years—one of the top salespeople in the country. Top five. Along comes the dreaded Acquisition and Merger Monster, sprinkles a little New Policy dust around after the merger, and my friend gets an offer that works out to one half his usual commission plan . . . *After all, you do have a job. You know how many people don't? Thousands, pal. Maybe millions* . . . Then there are the poor starving children in Africa, but we don't need to get into that right now.

Outsourcing is another reason that The Rules Have Changed. *Forbes* magazine informs us that . . . *By the year 2002, seventy-five percent of the information technology within corporate America will be outsourced* . . . Companies don't want to build an infrastructure, don't want to add overhead, because costs will go up, pricing will have to go up, and they'll no longer by competitive. Remember how it was in sports during the so-called Golden Age? Mickey Mantle and Whitey Ford with the Yankees? Duke Snider with the Dodgers? (So Duke finished with the Giants. Big deal.) One-team guys. That's how business was.

Now, businesses (and sports franchises) that are poised for a timely strike at the Gold Ring will often go out and get some key people to ensure their success. The Hired Gun. Or Hired Guns. That's where you come in.

The Harvard Business School Press reminds us that . . . *Every successful organization will tell you that they have quadrupled turnover during the last ten years* . . . The whole scenario spells o-p-p-o-r-t-u-n-i-t-y. Was it better the old way? I don't know (though, as you might guess, I have some opinions). I do know that it was different. Now we have New Rules, and if we don't learn them, we're not going to be able to compete at all. We'll turn out to be nonfactors in the business world. Not a fun concept. Especially since it doesn't have to be that way.

So what do we know so far? We know that The Rules Have Changed, that Companies Have Changed, ergo (another great Harvard word in case you miss the dead language approach) that Career Paths Have Changed.

► ## JOB SECURITY IS A THING OF THE PAST ◄

It simply doesn't exist anymore. Even if you're willing to settle for 3 or 4 percent annual raises (please, O Great Pumpkin, let that be above the inflation rate), just when you're about ready to ease into that rocking chair routine, just when you think it's safe to go in the water again, some conglomerate will come along and acquire your company or merge with your company and—*zap!*—they'll have a whole new agenda that may not include you. So much for security.

People who are prospering today are people who are willing to take advantage of the opportunities, people who are willing to take a chance. Have you looked at the want ads in your local newspaper lately? Depending on the size of your city, there are most likely pages and pages of ads. There are industries that are having labor shortages: Information Technology, Telecommunications, Retail, Banking and Finance, Health and Medical (more about that in the next chapter).

Financial rewards are changing, too. I got a signing bonus at my last two jobs; that's not uncommon. If you stay a year, you may be in line for a retention bonus. Now is the time to be negotiating those kinds of things.

From 1945 to 1971, the economy grew incrementally every year and so did real family income. In the mid-seventies, when the global economy started to change (remember the oil crisis, etc.), growth flattened out and has not improved much since. There's been a big decline in the acceleration of the standard of living for the average U.S. citizen. Some have prospered, but overall that hasn't been true. Yet if you look at the profit picture of Corporate America during this period, you find a far different picture—Corporate Profits are rising rapidly while Wages are slowly sinking. As you can see, the worker is the one who has been negatively impacted.

Consider for a moment the possibility that Job Jumping just might be a Career Strategy, perhaps a strong Career Strategy. It's certainly been that way for me. If the idea is foreign to you, just let it settle for a while. By the time you finish this book, it may seem a whole lot more attractive.

An article in *Fortune* magazine dated April 1996 addressed the whole issue of right-sizing, down-sizing, etc.:

> *When will down-sizing end? Never. Get used to it. It's part of the new economy, the new rule.*

Never? That may be a long time . . .

A survey by the American Management Association revealed that 60 percent of the companies surveyed stated that they would eliminate jobs over the next year. That's the highest percentage in survey history.

Is your job one of those?

On the other hand, managerial employment

has increased three times as fast as overall employment (which has posted minuscule gains in the past
year). When companies move from cost-cutting
strategies to growth strategies, they need people
with management skills. That's also called an
o-p-p-o-r-t-u-n-i-t-y.

Listen to what Harry S. Dent Jr. (author of
The Great Boom Ahead) says about all this:

> *Most of our organizations are in for changes
> more radical than their leadership ever
> dreamed. They won't be optional or gradual,
> they'll be sweeping, swift and certainly posi-
> tively mandated by economic and technolog-
> ical changes. We need to understand change
> and make it our ally.*

According to the Yankee Group, consulting
services throughout business will grow to $116 bil-
lion in sales by the year 2000. That's *b* as in *breath-
taking*. Allan Sinai, president of a prominent
research firm, has this to say about the job market:

> *This is a huge, huge revolution, like the ad-
> vent of the railroads and air travel . . .*

Lest I bore you to death with quotes and statistics,
I leave you with a few thoughts before we enter

the next step in our journey. If you're performing a noncore (noncritical) function, the chances of your job being outsourced and you being re-engineered or neutered (ouch!) are excellent. Be aware of that. Companies are now immersed in a quickly changing business environment brought on by, among other things, the pressures of a global economy. That's just the way things are. But we need to understand that and be able to position ourselves with the right company, negotiate the right deal and take advantage of the situation. O-p-p-o-r-t-u-n-i-t-y.

If nothing else, you'll certainly know how to spell *opportunity* by the time you're through with this book.

In the following chapters we will discuss strategies about how to be in the right place at the right time, how to pick the right industry, how to market yourself, how to interview, all the things you need to take advantage of the New Rules.

"BIG RAISE"
STRATEGIES

▸ The fundamental business rules are changing rapidly.

▸ Companies must put themselves in a position to change and respond to their market quickly.

▸ The company's loyalty to you can change overnight (due to many factors).

▸ You and I, the working stiffs, can greatly benefit from the New Rules by developing a Job Jumping career strategy.

▸ Change! Change! Change!

2

GET IN THE RIGHT INDUSTRY AND GET THE RIGHT JOB

or
"Toto, I Have a Feeling We're Not in Kansas Anymore!"

Now on to the nuts and bolts.
The choices are:

1. You can be like Dilbert and his buddies and stay miserable in the same old job.
2. You can do what I did—change jobs four times in the last five years—and reap the financial rewards.
3. Sorry, there's no Door Number 3.

And since you, Noble Reader, don't know me from Adam, now is a good time to put my cards on the table and give you a brief rundown on my job adventures and the subsequent financial windfalls that have occurred during the last five years . . . Because (be honest now) isn't the prospect of more money what got you interested in this book in the first place?

1992—$48K+. Company: Haworth
1993—(Change #1) $65K+. Company: Vanstar
1994—(Change #2) $90K+. Company: Entex
1996—(Change #3) $120K+. Company: En-Pointe
1997—(Change #4) $140K+. Company: Core-Tech

If you connect the dots, you'll see that the line goes up and to the right. You remember all those overhead slides you saw with company profits headed that way? Remember how pleased everyone seemed to be? Now it's your turn.

> ► **FIRST THING TO DO IS IDENTIFY THE INDUSTRIES THAT ARE GOING TO SHOW STRONG GROWTH IN THE NEXT TEN YEARS. THAT'S WHERE YOU WANT TO BE** ◄

A recent *Business Week* article lists the industries where the best jobs will be. Information Technology (something of an umbrella classification that includes Telecommunications, Computer Science, all kinds of High Tech) tops the list, with Health Care, Retail/Wholesale, Robotics, Finance and Education not far behind. Another article in the same magazine states that over 50 percent of the management jobs that will be available will be in High Tech and Education. Over 50 percent . . . Let that sink in for a minute . . . What we see unfolding is a labor shortage in certain industries, a simple supply-and-demand situation that we can use to our advantage.

The Bureau of Labor lists the following high-demand positions and projected number of openings for the time period 1994–2005:

Teachers—660,000 openings
Nurses—470,000
Executives—466,000
Truck drivers—271,000
Financial managers—192,000
Accountants—120,000
Social workers—121,000.

Shouldn't one of those openings belong to you?

Look at those want ads we talked about in the last chapter. Pages of Computer Science jobs, Health/Medical jobs, Banking/Finance jobs, Education jobs and more. We want to identify growth industries that will provide us with more job opportunities and higher wages, with a playing field that is slanted in our direction for a change. Here you'll have to do your homework. (You didn't really think this was some kind of deal where I waved a magic wand and you got a better job, did you? Of course not. I knew you were smarter than that.)

A good place to start (if you are not electronically challenged) is the computer and a good on-line search. Some helpful hints:

- Try SkillSearch (www.recruiting-links.com). Employers from all over are posting jobs and employment information on their Web sites. SkillSearch will help you search for jobs based on preferred industries, location or job title. A free e-mail service will alert you to job postings that match your preferences.
- Career Resource Center (www.careers.org) bills itself as "The Internet's most complete and extensive index of career-related Web sites."
- Career Web (www.cweb.com) provides more of the same, with a slightly different format.
- Career Path (www.careerpath.com) is a personal favorite.

Another reliable old standby is your local library. (Yes, Virginia, there are still things called books, with real pages that contain information and entertainment. There will always be books because it's too hard to curl up with a computer in your lap on a snowy night.) Look at business periodicals, e.g., *Forbes,* October 1997—"200 Best Small Companies in the U.S." Stay informed and stay up to date.

Now that you have identified the growth industries, there are several types of companies within those industries that you want to target. Companies that are highly profitable (Intel, Microsoft, etc.) will often be willing to pay higher wages for the right people (you). Staying current with business periodicals like *Fortune, Forbes, Inc.* and *Business Week* will help you identify them. Companies that outsource (thereby saving dollars) have a tendency to pay more for permanent employees.

Look for companies that are willing to "share the wealth" by encouraging employees to "create value." In the summer of 1997 I went to work as a district manager for the CoreTech Consulting Group, a privately owned company that does about $50,000,000 a year in computer consulting services. There are several reasons I chose them:

1. It's a company in a growth industry (Information Technology is growing at a rate of better than 20 percent a year, while the U.S. average is 4.5 percent).
2. They're highly profitable.
3. They're willing to "share the wealth" by helping to create value.

And why would they want to do that? (Thanks for the question. I always need a good straight man to keep things moving. Or straight woman.) When they go public (an initial public offering, or IPO), they stand to get twenty to twenty-five times their annual earnings. Microsoft was one of the first companies to do that. They gave employees stock options, encouraged people to work long hours, to believe that they were an integral part of the company and that if the company profited, the employees would also. Another example of the old bromide *A high tide raises all boats.* Corny but true. So what happened at Microsoft? When the stock went public, a quarter of their employees became millionaires literally overnight. There are lots of companies that do that now, and they are not all High Tech.

At CoreTech, all the employees are given equity shares. Some are given executive stock options, which essentially means that as the market value of the company increases, I get a piece of the action. If the company achieves its five-year goals, I stand to make a considerable amount of money. We're talking serious money here . . . Am I interested in CoreTech's success? You bet I am.

Many firms have adopted their own versions of "share the wealth." One such company developed the Self-Directed Work Team concept in hopes of finding ways to reduce cost and increase revenue. If teams can come up with cost-reducing/revenue-increasing plans, they are rewarded. Not comp time and a hug. Real money . . . If you are part of the solution, companies will pay for it. And you know what? It works. The Lowe's Companies gave each of their employees stock shares as an incentive to improve profits. Low profit, low stock value. High profit . . . You can figure it out. Guess what? The stock value has increased eightfold in the last six years. Management has finally come to the realization that if employees have a real stake in company success, if how much money they make is tied to how much money the company makes, they tend to be more focused and interested in that success. This is just simple arithmetic, not brain surgery.

In 1993 I was employed at Haworth, a billion-dollar-plus-a-year, high-end office furniture manufacturer. I was the territorial sales manager, with a multistate territory. It's a great company and I had a great job. But I wasn't going anywhere. The company had about as much market share as it was going to get. The industry was growing at only 5 percent a year, so the company wasn't willing to pay the big money anymore. Tops would maybe have been something like $70,000. Another simple arithmetic problem; you don't even need a calculator for this kind. From a financial standpoint, the job was a virtual dead end. Don't get me wrong, there's nothing wrong with $70,000 a year. But if there are other opportunities (and there are), why not pursue them?

WHAT TO DO

1. You need to assess your strengths and determine what industries are a good fit. What do I do well? What do I bring to the table? How am I going to bring the most value?
2. Next, you need to identify growth industries and then pick companies within those industries that are changing rapidly, companies that "share the wealth," companies that are highly profitable. And don't worry too much about technical expertise. As the following story illustrates, my overwhelming lack of technical know-how hasn't slowed my progress in the least in the job market.

Entex is a PC systems integrator company with somewhere in the neighborhood of $2 billion a year in sales. Here in Denver they employ about four hundred people. Shortly after I hired on as the branch manager, we had our Christmas party; at the party they gave a prize for the Least Technical Person. And of course I won. There is a certain irony in having the branch manager at a High Tech company win the Least Technical Person Award.

In those days, I didn't have a clue. I had to ask

my secretary every hour or so to come in and help me reboot my computer. It didn't make me a poor manager or a poor organizer and it didn't stop me from being successful—and it won't stop you. It just meant that I didn't know much about computers. Yet. My strengths have to do with developing sales teams, planning, writing and implementing business strategies.

Remember:

> ► **IDENTIFY YOUR STRENGTHS AND CHASE JOBS THAT PLAY TO THEM** ◄

Let's do a little summarizing about the Right Industry and the Right Job. Ted Koppel recently did an entire segment on *Nightline* on the labor shortage in High Tech (right industry). *Business Week* did a long article on the same thing. But this phenomenon is not limited just to High Tech. There are many other industries with the same problem, and the list is growing each day. If you do your research, it's easy to find out which ones they are. So what does all of this spell? O-p-p-o-r-t-u-n-i-t-y.

Look for companies within rapidly growing industries that "share the wealth," that give stock options, that encourage employees to think as entrepreneurs, that "create value."

A few examples of companies that meet those criteria are:

Nike
Dayton Hudson
Gallup
Massachusetts Mutual
Southwest Airlines
Starbucks
Harley-Davidson
USAA

Now that you have compiled a list of growth industries and jobs within those industries, and you have assessed your strengths, you're ready to move ahead.

"BIG RAISE"
STRATEGIES

▸ Do your research to determine the right industries to be in.

▸ Remember, your skills *can and will* transfer to a new and different industry.

▸ Locate companies that believe in "sharing the wealth."

▸ Identify your strengths.

▸ Go to work for a company that encourages you to think as an entrepreneur, and play to your strengths.

▸ Research! Research! Research!

3

WHEN TO START
LOOKING

or
Don't Go the Way of
Muhammad Ali

If you're not convinced of the soundness of what I'm saying after the first two chapters, close the book and return it to the bookstore. Tell them you were really looking for *Chicken Soup for the Teenage Soul* and you picked this book up by mistake. Look contrite—that always helps.

BUT if you are, if not convinced, at least a little curious, more evidence awaits you in the following chapters. Or, as Shakespeare might have said, "Read on, Macduff."

Kate Wendleton, president of the Five O'Clock Club, a career management organization based in New York, reports that she's seen compensation climb in the last year:

> There really is a wonderful market out there. People are leaving their employers and getting jobs so fast it makes your head spin. And they're getting enormous raises, too."

Times Have Never Been Better!!!

So what if you're happy with your present job? Things couldn't be better. It's a dream come true.

My recommendation? Be careful of the dreaded false sense of security. A good friend of mine was with the same company for twenty-eight years. He loved it! He couldn't have been happier. Then, one Monday morning, he got the word that his company was moving from Denver to New York City. He was dumbfounded, blindsided and bushwhacked. He didn't see it coming.

The Big Picture is this:

If you don't start thinking about a Career Strategy, you'll more than likely be left behind in the same old rut. And, as a friend of mine is fond of saying: *The only difference between the rut and the grave is a matter of depth* . . . You'll probably still have a job, but prosperity will be as elusive as ever.

Of course, switching jobs involves a fear factor. Perfectly normal. (Courage is acting in the face of fear, not being without fear.) Old Messages about loyalty and devotion to business are very powerful. You do your part and your employer will take care of you . . . Ho . . . Ho . . . Ho . . . That's a story that would be better prefaced with *One upon a time* . . . Strictly fairy-tale material in today's business climate.

Our parents or grandparents were the people who either lived through or were directly affected by the Great Depression. They thought of a job as a JOB. A big deal. Companies loved—and still love—that. They like you to be grateful. If you're grateful to just have a job, you're not likely to be pushing for higher wages or better working conditions. As a result, when Corporate Profits continue to go Up, Real Wages often either go Down or just stay flat (which is, of course, the same thing as going down).

To get a better salary, I made companies pay me what I was worth by my constantly changing jobs and testing the market. You think I didn't panic the first time I was about to change jobs? Guess again. Panic city. My wife thought it was the dumbest thing she'd ever heard of. (Now all she says is, *"Honey, just let me know when the insurance coverage changes."* Everyone I knew said, *"This is crazy, Gordon. You've got a good job with a secure future, why would you want to"* . . . et-cetera . . . All true. I did have a good job with a secure future. But I saw myself doing something else, having a bigger job, taking on more responsibility, making more money (maybe the order ought to be reversed).

Me, I'm a dreamer. I dreamed about taking it to the next level. When as formidable an intellect as Albert Einstein informs us, *"Imagination is more important than knowledge,"* who am I to argue? William James (you know, Henry's brother) wrote, *"The greatest discovery of my generation is that you can alter your life by altering your attitude."* Remember: The Rules Have Changed. *"Don't cross the road, Gordon"* was really good advice when I was three years old. When I got to be thirty and was still afraid to cross the road, it wasn't such great advice. Perhaps you need to think about altering some of the same old attitudes you grew up with.

So I took a chance. Not a BIG chance, mind you. Just a little chance. I began trolling the waters. There could be jobs out there. Maybe even a BIG job. Somebody had to get those jobs. Why couldn't it be me? But I'd never know if I didn't throw my hook into the water. That's the start. You don't have to run off and join the circus, sell everything you own and go into business for yourself. You just have to be willing to throw the hook into the water. Very simple. Throw-hook-into-water. There, how hard was that?

The January 1998 issue of *Kiplinger's Personal Finance Magazine* states:

> *Demand is strong for skilled workers with college-level training. At some point, firms will be forced to bid up wages to keep or ac-*

quire top employees . . . From a small busi-ness perspective, the question is not whether we can grow but whether we can find the people to staff the growth.

Sounds like the *o* word again to me. (No, not that *o* word!) Now, the opportunity isn't going to go away next week or next month. It will be around for a while. But the sooner you take advantage of it, the better the chances for capitalizing on it.

When do you start looking?

Now.

When things are good.

When you're a hero.

The tendency is to wait until the downward slide begins. Don't. You and everybody else will be out looking for the same job.

▶ **START LOOKING WHEN YOU'RE AT THE TOP OF YOUR GAME, WHEN THINGS HAVE NEVER BEEN BETTER** ◀

I left Haworth after sales had doubled in eighteen months. I left Vanstar after sales had doubled in a year. I left Entex after we had just won an $80,000,000 project (I can't resist all those zeroes).

I made my exit from EnPointe after sales had quadrupled in twelve short months.

When do you *not* start looking? Don't start looking just because you're mad at your boss or you can't get your own key to the executive washroom. Leave when you're ready. Don't be driven out by a personality conflict—leave on your own terms. If it's too soon, you'll have no track record. If it's too late, well, maybe you end up like Muhammad Ali, a few bouts too many and you don't have much punch or razzle-dazzle left. The "times" may have passed you by.

Over the years I've hired dozens of people. Many of the choice prospects that I really wanted wouldn't leave their present jobs (even for higher wages and a better deal) because a) *Hey, things are great,* or b) *Hey, I'm on top.* The New Rules say, *Hey, leave when things are great.* I'm not proposing this as an ideal to be applied to marriage or your bowling league. But in the business world, it works. Leave after the 20-win season or when you're hitting .312, not when your ERA is drifting up into the 5 or 6 range or when your batting average is hovering around the Mendoza Line. Teams/businesses want you when you're at the top of your game (see Chapter 4, "How to Market Yourself").

ALWAYS BE LOOKING FOR OPPORTUNITIES

The Victims of the New Economy are those who live in a state of perpetual anxiety and fear about what's going to happen to their jobs. If the rumors are flying at your company, if everybody is rushing to the bank to cash payday checks, you should already be looking—staying will be detrimental to your financial and emotional health. You have absolutely nothing to lose by going out to test the job market. Nothing. Nada. Zip. You'll be more relaxed and at ease because you already have a job. Food and shelter are not big problems—the haunted look of the chronically unemployed is not seeping relentlessly through your smile. A toe in the water is a good start; you don't have to jump off the deep end. You'll be amazed at what you'll find.

This is what *Business Horizons* magazine has to say about the current turmoil and its effect on employees:

> *One explanation for the steady growth of mental health problems over the last twenty years is the increased pressure, pace and un-*

certainty of modern business life . . . Lots of companies went through downsizing; an incredible number of takeovers, buyouts and mergers took place. The impact on the worker has been very unsettling.

Amen, I say. And the best way to get out of depression, anxiety and uncertainty over our jobs is to Take Action.

When?

Now.

Why?

The Rules Have Changed.

*B*ecause companies have to bring out new products, explore new markets, advertise differently, be able to change literally overnight, they are looking for new kinds of employees—people who can be "change agents."

Remember, changing jobs is a Career Strategy, not a random business reaction to the fact that you're unhappy. It is a positive, proactive choice.

"BIG RAISE"
STRATEGIES

- ▶ Think of Job Jumping as a Career Strategy.

- ▶ Don't stay in your present job too long. You hurt your chances to prosper under the New Rules.

- ▶ Leave your present job when you are "on top," when things are good.

- ▶ Always be looking for the next opportunity, even though you may not actually plan to change jobs immediately.

- ▶ Plan! Plan! Plan!

4

HOW TO MARKET YOURSELF

or
This Little Piggy Went to Market, This Little Piggy Stayed Home (Guess Who Made Out Best?)

Money Market, March 1995:

Key job skills for the future are soft/skill oriented; they include an ongoing appetite for change, being comfortable with fast decision making, the ability to manage and motivate yourself.

While the above qualities are invaluable, perhaps most important of all, if you're going to be a player in the new business environment, you must develop the ability to market yourself. I know that may not seem attractive; self-promotion may not seem like the American Way to do things. After all, would John Wayne and Gary Cooper have marketed themselves?

Of course they would have. And did, as a matter of fact. You're two strikes down if you go into this thing with your hat in your hand. In fact, I have found that marketing yourself may be the key differentiator between you and your competitor for a position.

To Market, to Market, to Market We Go . . .

That's better.

Now that you have identified the right industry and several of the right companies that most assuredly will appreciate and reward your considerable talents, how do you go about marketing yourself?

BUILD A REPUTATION WITHIN YOUR COMPANY

The first thing you must do is establish a reputation for performance within your present company. If you can't do that, you can forget about moving up the ladder. If you can't do that, you can probably forget about your present job, too. It'll just be a matter of time before you'll be discovered as a Slug and summarily dismissed. Nobody needs Slugs . . . Nobody.

Make sure that people in the company know about the positive things you've accomplished. This is not meant to be an ego trip, and will be at best counterproductive if it is perceived as such. You don't want that. Simply let people know.

The first year I was with Haworth, I was the number two salesman in the western half of the

United States (two out of seventy-four). I didn't run around and tell people, *Hey, look at Me! Did I do a great job or what?* Didn't have to. I made sure that I thanked all the people who helped me—people in Finance, Credit, Contracts, everyone. They truly did make it happen, and thanking them served two purposes.

First, it made them feel as though they were an important part of the process (which they were), and second, it helped spread the word that I had had a terrific year If you tell people what a great job *they* are doing, even those who are not doing such a great job will more than likely try to live up to your expectations (or the expectations of their peers). They in turn will tell others what a great job *you* are doing. Internal marketing is very important. It never hurts to advertise if you have a great product. And having other people do it makes it doubly effective. Always treat everyone with respect.

*O*ther strategies for internal marketing include serving on committees, writing articles for the company periodical, volunteering for presentations, helping other employees be good at their jobs. Winners like to do business with winners. I like my name to come up when people mention winners. It all helps to build your reputation within the company.

When people leave and go to other companies, it doesn't hurt to have your name mentioned in a positive way by people you've worked with. That's the best kind of marketing. When I went from Haworth to Vanstar, they hired me primarily because of my success at Haworth. I didn't have to tell them I'd been successful; other people did that for me. When I went from Vanstar to Entex, it was the same story. I left Vanstar at the top of my game, just having won a big contract at MCI. I went from Entex to EnPointe just after winning a multi-million-dollar deal with US West. I left EnPointe for CoreTech after quadrupling sales in one year. In each case, a number of people from my previous company and/or associates within the industry had spread the word that I had done a good job.

Gary Grappo, in his book *The Top 10 Career Strategies for the Year 2000 and Beyond,* has this to say about the subject:

> *Learn to sell yourself like a company sells a product . . . Why? Because of the competition, inside and outside.*

Don't make the mistake of overselling. If you're doing your job right, others will promote your name. When it comes time for the actual interview (see Chapter 5), dress well and look the part. That may seem almost too obvious, but you'd be surprised at the number of people who don't do it.

DEVELOP A MINI–BUSINESS PLAN

Before a job interview, develop a Mini–Business Plan for the position you are applying for, one that says, *If you hire me, this is what I'll do for your company.* Include sales or operational strategies, account management, how to reduce problems, streamline processes, what you would do to correct some perceived shortcomings (be diplomatic with this last suggestion). A one- or two-page overview. Nothing fancy. Just put it down in black and white. In all probability, the prospective employer will not ask you to submit one; you'll have to take the initiative and do it on your own.

When I was interviewing with Entex, I sent a one-page business plan highlighting what I would do if I was given the position. The VP of Sales, with whom I was interviewing, liked it so much he asked me to present it to another person on his team. Companies are looking for someone who will have an immediate impact. By doing a Mini–Business Plan, you will have given them some assurance that you can produce results. And I guarantee you they will be impressed. Guarantee it.

And while we're at it, here's my perspective on resumes. (I know you didn't ask, but here it is anyway.) There's a ton of software available to enable people to write a very professional resume. Get a program and do it right. Make it clean and professional. Some software allows you to do your resume in color. Rainbows and roses. Catch the eye, get the attention . . . Forget it. It's not the way to go. Stick to the basics. Besides, a resume is not going to get you the job. That's the role of the interview and the Mini–Business Plan.

I've done a substantial amount of hiring at my last three jobs (probably hired in excess of a hundred people), and I always want to know what Mr. or Mrs. Prospect has accomplished lately and what he or she is going to do for me today. Right now. And how he or she is going to accomplish it. That's what a Mini–Business Plan does. And this is not just for high-profile jobs. It can, and does, work in fields as diverse as Health Care or Car Sales.

My son Brett, fresh out of college, went from being a distributor for Russell Stover Candies to greeting card salesman to what, being a car nut, he had always wanted to be—car salesman. During the process, I helped him write a Mini–Business Plan . . . *Here's how I'd be a top salesman. Here's what I bring to the table that will help your company. Here are some ideas on marketing strategy, etc. . . .* And he got the job. (Which you already knew because if he hadn't, you knew I wouldn't have bothered telling the story.) He's nearly tripled his salary in four short years. A chip off the old block. Not bad for somebody who's not yet twenty-six years old. Believe me, it's not brain surgery, folks. Just common sense.

Miller and Heiman, in their book on Conceptual Selling, embrace the concept of using a coach during the sales process to let you know how you're doing, to monitor your progress, to gather information normally not available to you. The same holds true for marketing yourself. Periodic Reality Checks never hurt. Use colleagues or people outside the company, neighbors or fellow church-goers. They often have information not normally available to you. And information is power. We've all seen that at work.

The idea that people who change jobs frequently are undesirable is an Old, Old concept. If your track record is good, they are nothing short of absolutely eager to have you aboard. It's all part of the Top Gun Theory. What do I need to win TODAY? Because if I don't win today, there probably won't be a tomorrow. The business world is now a constant pennant race. All the marbles on the table every day. Check the bottom line at noon. Check it again at five (or six or seven), when you go home.

We may feel that the pace is too frantic (which it is), that we're all working ourselves into early graves (possibly true), but this is the way the Game is played today. Maybe not forever, but at least today. You wanna play? Then check out the New Rules.

The truth is that companies look favorably on what I sometimes call Job Jumpers. They often bring new ideas, new information, new strategies to the table that long-term employees don't have access to. What's the competition doing? Your latest hire may just know. Job Jumping is a positive. The benefit is short-term impact. Companies don't like to view you as a project, someone who will take two years to get up to speeeeeed to make a c-o-n-t-r-i-b-u-t-i-o-n. They like you to hit the ground running . . . Make it one of your goals to have something happen within the first ninety days, something positive that will be visible. If you bring talented people with you, that's a definite plus. The cost of hiring or replacing an employee is equal to one year's salary. A substantial outlay.

So if you can come in with a team, or part of a team, for the pennant drive, so much the better. When the pennant drive is over, when Phase III or Phase IV is finished for that particular company, they may not need you anymore. That's okay. If they don't, somebody else will. Your reputation will have preceded you.

Now, all bets are off if you're doing a lousy job. You do a lousy job, you will probably get what you deserve. Which may be nothing. This book is not for people doing substandard work. (It's probably still not too late to take the book back. I mean, if you haven't spilled coffee on it. If you have, you can forget the story about *Chicken Soup for the Teenage Soul.*)

The people who do the actual hiring like to look good, too. If you make an impact, they in turn look like geniuses. It never hurts to make people look good. By the same token, it never, ever helps to make people look bad. Ever. It will always come back to haunt you. A very old principle states, *What you offer, you receive.* (That's a takeoff on the old Biblical injunction *As you sow, so shall you reap.*)

Professional recruiters (Headhunters) provide additional avenues to explore. Make yourself known to some of them. They'll spread the word around. If they get you a job and you have a positive impact, they look good. The better they look, the more business they do, the more money they make. Ain't Capitalism wonderful? See how it works?

"BIG RAISE"
STRATEGIES

▸ Marketing yourself is not a negative or difficult task.

▸ You don't have to be a "sales type" to be good at marketing yourself.

▸ Start by developing a positive reputation for performance with your current employer.

▸ Treat everyone with the utmost respect.

▸ Before an interview, develop a one- or two-page Mini–Business Plan detailing how you are going to: bring value to your new employer, fix problems they have, open new markets for them, improve efficiencies, etc., etc.

▸ Get a coach to monitor the process.

▸ To Market! To Market! To Market!

5

HOW TO WIN THE RIGHT JOB

or
Interviewing for Fun and Profit

The view from the top.

When you're already in a good position (you have a job you don't hate, the pay is acceptable, the working conditions okay), you're negotiating from a position of strength. My attitude was always *So what if I don't get the job?* . . . I'm in the driver's seat. It's the perfect Win/Win Situation we always look for. The old saying *It's always easier to get a job when you have a job* is certainly true. Confidence is the key. Since I was doing a good job for the company I was with, I had absolutely nothing to lose (and perhaps a great deal to gain).

There are literally hundreds of books available on How to Interview Effectively, How to Write a Winning Resume, How to Get the Job of Your Dreams (you writers out there will be familiar with the books on How to Write a Winning Query Letter). So what's so hot about this chapter? What sort of edge can I give you? As always, it's the little things.

- *Edge:* Interview at your best time of day. I'm no good in the late afternoon. I get up at 4 A.M.

to have some quiet time, run for a bit, maybe hit the health club; by late afternoon I'm practically out of gas. Sluggish. Toast. Slow on the uptake. I'm better in the morning. Lots better. I'm also more confident and feel better about myself after a workout at the gym. So I try to set up my interviews for midmorning. It's just a fact that at certain times of the day you'll be better. Knowing that gives you an edge.

- *Edge:* Don't always defer to the prospective company (remember, you have a job and you're doing quite well, thank you); let them know what times you're available. I have also canceled interviews because something has come up with a customer that needs my attention. Or maybe it's a new project. But customer concerns are the best. That says to the interviewer that I am very concerned with customer satisfaction. This is how I deal with that. And not even this Golden Opportunity with Company XYZ is more important than the customer. Companies like the idea that you put the customer first. They've been preaching it for years without much success, and all of a sudden you show up out of the blue with the very lesson they've been trying to teach.

- *Edge:* Tell the company what you're going to do for them. Doesn't that make sense? Wouldn't you rather hire somebody who was interested in adding value to the company than somebody who was wondering what you were going to do for him or her? Since I am much more often the interviewer rather than the interviewee (Is that a word? Interviewee?), I am amazed at how often people want to know what the company is going to do for *them.* Is this a Generation X thing? Baby Boomer stuff maybe? What I do know is that it's a very poor interview tactic (and I bet nine out of ten people still do it). That doesn't mean you can't ask questions about the direction of the company, the vision, etc., but don't make your interest in salary and benefit considerations the main topic of discussion. If you're interviewing with me, I'll guarantee it will be a short interview.

• *Edge:* Don't wait for the interviewer to ask what you're bringing to the table. Set your agenda in place before the *Why should we hire you?* question comes up. When I went from Entex to EnPointe, a few of the things I put in my Mini–Business Plan were what accounts I was familiar with, what I thought my success ratio in bringing in new business would be, what other prospects I had. I planned to bring two salespeople and an inside support person with me when I hired on. That would be a significant saving for EnPointe. Recent research indicates that the cost of hiring a person is somewhere in the $30,000-to-$50,000 range (depending on the type and duration of training he or she receives). There's lost productivity, as well as downtime and general friction in the system, which slows everything down for a time.

- *Edge:* Present and reinforce your Mini–Business Plan. It's a great way to market yourself. Be specific . . . *Here's what I'm going to do in the first thirty days, the second thirty days, etc.* . . . Lay it out.

- *Edge:* Take awards, commendations, etc., with you to the interview. It's concrete evidence that you can perform as advertised. When I interviewed with Vanstar, I took copies of awards I had won at Haworth, letters from customers saying what a great job I'd done, an award as the Best New Business Developer. All good stuff. When I went from Vanstar to Entex, I took recaps of what I had accomplished; from Entex to EnPointe, my President's Club Award (the actual plaque), copies of a company magazine article detailing the $80,000,000 contract I had helped win with US West.

- *Edge:* Think of yourself as a Change Agent. Change is rampant in all sectors of the business world. The ability to change on the proverbial dime is no longer a luxury. Being big and powerful (and clumsy and unable to change quickly) almost killed IBM. And a number of others. Companies like people who endorse change, embrace change, people who bring new ideas about how to stay ahead of the competition. You need to talk about that during the interview. Remember that you already have a great position.

You're not going to drink hemlock if you don't get this job. So take some risks in the interview. Be proactive . . . *Here are some ideas that I believe will put us ahead of the competition* . . . They don't have to be perfect ideas. Just ideas. Talk about what you're going to do for *them.* Give some examples. Don't just ask about the benefit package and wait for them to crown you with a laurel wreath because you have a wonderful smile. Plenty of time for that after you've sold yourself, after you've convinced them that they can't possibly get along without you.

Having said all that, there are legitimate questions that you can ask . . . *What's the vision for the company over the next four to five years? Where are they going? Do they have a strategy that encourages employee participation in decision making?*

Before the sometimes thorny question of *Why have you been with so many companies during the last five years?* even comes up, I tell them what a wealth of experience I bring as someone who has worked for their competitors. I know what they're doing. Having been with four Information Technology companies in the last five years, I developed a vision for that field. And I have brought that broader vision with me. Sometimes long-term employees lose that competitive edge; people often get tunnel vision after working for the same company for a number of years. Not a criticism, just a fact.

- *Edge:* Do your homework, your research. Use your network and coaches to find out what areas the company you're interviewing with may not be doing so well in. Perhaps sales are great but they're struggling with customer support. Talk about the fact that you bring strength where they may be weak. I'm always impressed when people have done their research. Others will be, too.

- *Edge:* Remember that the interview is give-and-take. Think of it as auditioning for a part in a movie. If you're auditioning for Attila the Hun, don't come dressed like Mary Poppins. Or acting like Mary Poppins. If you're interviewing for a sales job, bring to that role, that audition, the experience, knowledge and depth that you have acquired. Dress the part. Act the part. If you're interviewing for a teaching job, remember not to come dressed as Attila the Hun (unless maybe it's in the inner city—then the Attila outfit may be just the thing they're looking for). So if you dress the part and act the part, you get the part.

Get it?

Toward the end of the interview (don't worry, you'll know when it's ending), I like to ask the interviewer what concerns he or she has about me. Some will be honest and open (information you can use for future interviews), some will not. Either way, I like to ask. If nothing else, it at least demonstrates that I'm willing to face any objections the interviewer may have.

PRACTICE INTERVIEWING

That's right, practice interviewing! Find someone who does interviewing (doesn't have to be in your company), buy him (or her) lunch or a drink and find out what he asks people during interviews, what he likes to hear, etc. Find someone to actually interview you and then give you a critique on your performance.

If You Don't Interview Well, You Don't Get the Part (or At Least the Good Part) . . .

It's not philosophy, just simple fact.

In conclusion, remember:

The time is right for winning that great position.

Stock options, start-up bonuses, retention bonuses—all are available for the asking.

Keep in mind that this is not just about getting-a-job. Nearly anybody can get a job. The unemployment rate is now (1998) lower than it's been in years. This is about getting that great position you've always wanted.

Once you've changed companies, how can you have an immediate impact on the company you go to? Funny you should ask. That's what Chapter 6 is all about.

"BIG RAISE"
STRATEGIES

- ▶ Interview at the time of day when you are at your peak.

- ▶ Save the "what can the company do for me" question for the last.

- ▶ Focus on what you can do for the company (is that a Kennedyism?).

- ▶ Present your Mini–Business Plan.

- ▶ Take awards, past commendations, etc., to the interview.

- ▶ Address right away (before they ask) why you have changed jobs in the past; state that you were "fiercely loyal" to your previous employers.

- ▶ Present! Present! Present!

6

HOW TO HAVE A
POSITIVE IMPACT

or
How to Be Noticed Without
Being Obnoxious

THINK OF A JOB AS NO MORE THAN A THREE- TO FOUR-YEAR PROPOSITION

Now that you see the merits of frequent job changes (you do, don't you? Please say yes), you'll need to think differently about how long you're going to be on the job and how that mind-set will play into the way you approach your work.

The old thinking was Long-Term Stability. That's gone the way of the buggy whip. More recently, perhaps, but gone nonetheless. Years ago big companies put new employees in one-year, two-year or even three-year training programs. That strategy also went out about the same time the bottom dropped out of the buggy whip market. I personally think in a time frame of a year to a year and a half. I'm not advocating that for everyone, but three to four years is a realistic time frame. Certainly no more than that (unless you've fallen in love with the company and they've made you president for life).

To position yourself for the next job, you want to have an immediate impact, whether you are a secretary or a vice president; whether you are in the area of finance, maintenance, customer service or sales. Obviously an immediate *positive* impact. You remember those plaques and letters we talked about presenting during interviews? How important they were? You want to keep those coming. Three-year-old commendation letters are ancient history. They're worse than ancient history because there actually are people interested in ancient history. But nobody in the business world will be interested in ancient commendation letters. *Nobody.* People will want to know what you have contributed to the dynamic, exciting world of business lately. As in *recently.* That's not an unreasonable expectation.

One way to have an immediate positive impact is to find yourself taking the place of someone who was previously unsuccessful. This is the best of all situations and makes your chances of looking like a HERO much better. When I went to work at Haworth, I took over a multistate territory that had not been successful. A perfect situation. By the end of the first year I had achieved 150 percent of my goal.

Hero time.

If I were living in the (former) Soviet Union, I would have been given a medal. Here, better yet, I got a huge bonus. Keep in mind that while medals are nice and may be fun to display while marching in parades, money is the thing you want. Grocery stores no longer take medals as a medium of exchange. And really, how many parades do you march in anyway?

The same scenario played out for me at Vanstar. I took over in a situation where the patient was showing little signs of real life. I had nowhere to go but up.

Even when you are placed in a situation where things have been pretty good, there's always room for improvement. Just because the patient is still breathing doesn't mean he's healthy. Breathing is just breathing. In that case, find out what bothers top management. You'll need to be discreet, but it won't be a secret. Plenty of people will know. Find out what management didn't like about the way the position was run before you arrived. Focus on changing those things.

At Haworth they weren't happy with the sales

growth for the last three years. Plus the dealers weren't happy. The previous manager hadn't been able to deliver the goods, hence the reason they hired me—I had a proven track record of quickly growing sales. Vanstar and EnPointe were both looking for sales growth.

> ## TO HAVE AN IMPACT, LOOK FOR WHAT ISN'T WORKING AND FIX IT

Once you're on board and have had a chance to assess the situation, put together a thirty-day plan to address the issues. Go to management with it . . . *Here's what I'll be doing for the next thirty days. Any recommendations? . . .*

Keep management in the loop. Be sure to communicate with them. Overcommunicate if necessary. Send them information on everything you're doing.

Talk with dissatisfied customers as soon as possible. Don't avoid trouble; meet it head-on. Actively solicit management input on the most painful issues of the day. And don't forget fellow-employee insights; some of your most useful information will come from the troops on the front line.

If you need to make changes, make them quickly. Management loves it, customers love it, employees love it.

TO DEVELOP A WINNING TEAM, CLEAN HOUSE QUICKLY

It Is Not a Good Idea to Let Sub-par Employees Hang Around . . .

Not good for anyone, even the employee who is hanging around not doing anything with his/her life but (you guessed it) making life difficult for others. That's what bats do. Hang around. (Upside down in caves, I understand.) That might be okay for bats, but not for employees.

If you let them fly away, it does a number of things. First and most important, such a move changes the chemistry on the team to a more positive one. You'll find that even minor changes can make a great difference. It will convince team members you're serious about being successful. Customers will be grateful they don't have to deal with the turkey on your team anymore.

Entex had a multimillion-dollar-a-year contract with US West that was about to vanish into thin air because they were so unhappy with the kind of service they'd been getting. When I presented them with a ninety-day plan detailing changes we were going to make, they actually stood up and applauded. They were so excited that somebody was actually going to do something. What a concept. Action. As the comic strip hero says, WOW!

So make the changes quickly. Don't worry about upsetting the apple cart. Most people would like to see it upset more often. The tree will be a lot healthier if you cut off the dead branches from time to time. A friend of mine who works as a customer engineer at a major computer manufacturer tells the story of a deadbeat employee who was allowed to hang around for years, on and off probation, in and out of trouble with customers, not well liked by his fellow employees (because they were tired of carrying him and doing half his work), until one day a new and wonderful person showed up in Personnel, looked at his file and fired him. *"Dead wood,"* she said. *"Why is he still here?"* Good question. But why did it take so long?

I had the same experience at Vanstar. I had to fire someone who was absolutely dead weight. A millstone dragging everybody down. Previous management was afraid to let him go (for some weird reason). When I finally got him out the door, the other employees actually cheered.

This may sound like heresy, but some customers have to be cut off, too. There are those who provide no profit, no future, those who will always want more than you can reasonably provide and will just be a drain on resources. I tell them politely that we can't continue to do business with them on those terms. No hard feelings, but it's not a good fit. Just business. When I was with Vanstar, part of my thirty-day plan was to get rid of a certain customer. When I succeeded, I became an Instant Hero with the employees.

Don't be afraid to try out new ideas, especially if you're going into a situation where things aren't working.

Move people around. Some people have been in the same position for years and have gotten stale. They're good employees—show up every day, do their job—but they haven't had an interesting challenge in years. Some are simply going through the motions. Move them to a different job. In the business world they now call it Cross-Functional Training. Whatever you call it, it helps to start the creative juices flowing. Then again, some people may be suffering from good old-fashioned Burnout as a result of simmering in the same pan for years on end. Moving them will have a positive impact.

When things *do* start to change, deadbeat employees, marginal employees, whatever you want to call them, often tend to wash out by themselves. They'll stay as long as they're allowed to be marginal, but when they see that someone's coming in to shake things up with new ideas and a new philosophy, they'll sometimes do you a favor and leave by themselves.

Another big-impact move is to bring people with you when you move. That's a huge cost saving. They bring new ideas and a wealth of experience. And management loves it.

As part of my initial thirty-day plan at Vanstar, I had off-site meetings where we could talk freely. I asked for input . . . *These are the goals. How are we going to reach them?* . . . If you don't get the team to buy in, if they don't think they're an important part of the process, it won't make much difference what your goals are—you're probably not going to reach them anyway. But if they understand it's a "we" deal, stand back or you'll get run over.

At Vanstar we were doing $500,000 a month in sales. The goal was a $1,000,000 a month . . . *So*

how? I said. *I need help* . . . I assured everyone at
the meeting that there were no bad ideas. Or, to
put it another way, the only bad idea was having
no ideas. Let it flow. And they figured it out. I
knew they would.

We reviewed our progress every Monday at a
very short meeting . . . *Here's what we did last
week. How does it stack up? Are we on track to
meet our goals?* . . . Have enough metrics in the
system so you can measure progress with some ac-
curacy. Identify success factors. Measure against
them. *Send reports to management.*

Always keep bosses informed. Nobody likes
surprises and nobody likes to be blindsided. Managers least of all. If there is bad news on the hori-
zon (or already at the front door), let them know
now. Don't hide it and think it will somehow go
away. (Just because your head is in the sand doesn't
mean that other parts of you are not exposed.)
That's the Magic Wand approach . . . *I guess it's
gone, boss. I don't see it anymore* . . . Problems
don't typically solve themselves.

If you do go to your boss with a problem,
you will be expected to have some solution in
mind. The bottom line is that he will not lose confidence in you if you keep him informed.

Build relationships with top internal management. I built a good relationship with the number-two guy at Entex, and it paid off later: he gave me a solid reference when I was interviewing with CoreTech. You'd like them to be talking about you in a positive way. And of course they will be talking to other top-management people. More marketing. If you want to build a relationship with top management without stepping on the toes of those lower down in the food chain, send a note to your boss's boss telling him how great it is to work for your boss.

"BIG RAISE"
STRATEGIES

▸ Your goal is to have an immediate (thirty- to sixty-day) positive impact.

▸ Ideally, you'll be hired for a position in which the previous employee was unsuccessful.

▸ Look for management and customer service weaknesses and develop a thirty-day plan to fix them.

▸ Whenever possible, involve your team members in all important decisions.

▸ If you see trouble, present a proposal to management to solve it.

▸ Communicate! Communicate! Communicate!

7

THE PROOF IS IN THE PUDDING

or

*Get the Spoon Ready,
It's Time to Get into Action*

Many recent editions of newspapers and magazines support the strategy we've been discussing. A recent lead article in the *Denver Business Journal* states:

> TIGHT JOB MARKET GREETS THE FUTURE
> *Eighty-three percent of the employers polled believe the tight job market will continue well into the next century.*

The strategy I've been discussing will be valid for years to come. The business world has amply demonstrated that the Old Rules don't work. The New Rules dominate the business landscape.

Now, the strategy I've outlined is not for everyone. If it were, we'd have the most god-awful game of employment musical chairs imaginable. But from my own experience of changing jobs and talking to people during the last five years, I know there are a significant number of people for whom this is the perfect strategy. I was raised with the old work ethic. I'm the small-town Iowa guy. That ethic worked then, before the business climate and everything else started to accelerate so drastically. This particular strategy wasn't for me ten years ago.

But it takes time to rid ourselves of old messages, many that no longer apply. I think one of the ancient Greeks said, *All is changing save the law of change.* Maybe it was one of the Romans.

A professional recruiter named Hartman, in her book *Strategic Job-Jumping,* has this to say about being with a company for only a short period of time:

> *It's rare that anyone mentions it anymore. Used to be you wouldn't send a resumé if someone job hopped a lot, now it's a non-issue . . . And will be for years to come.*

Lest the picture seem too rosy, let me say that it is an issue with some people, so do your homework. Find rapidly changing companies that are growing, expanding . . . The talent pool is getting smaller and smaller and you'll be getting closer and closer to the top.

DON'T JUMP SHIP WITHOUT A PLAN

The almost certain result will be drowning.
As Hartman states in her book:

Are job jumpers easy to market? We try to find if clients have made intelligent choices throughout their career.

In his book *The Great Jobs Ahead,* Harry S. Dent Jr. says:

Instead of seeing downsizing and re-engineering as a threat, consider it the entrepreneurial opportunity of a lifetime.

"Entrepreneurial opportunity." That phrase is almost like poetry, isn't it? Since the big spike when the Baby Boomers started entering the job market, there have been fewer people in the skilled labor pool. In fact, there are 28 million fewer Gen Xers than Boomers. There are simply not enough people to go around. As I pointed out earlier, that spells o-p-p-o-r-t-u-n-i-t-y (it's been so long since we used that word, I thought you might have forgotten the spelling). Maybe bad for companies, but definitely good for us.

In the seventies the accepted mentality was *Don't rock the boat,* or *Be a good soldier.*

Message follows:

> ### DREAM BIG

Think outside the box. Use breakthrough thinking . . . *How can I bring value? How can I have an impact?* . . . Aim high. Only those with vision get the job of their dreams.

Newsday recently reported that

> *An important futuristic career skill is the ability to make job changes in a time of corporate downsizing and little job security.*

In the "What's In & What's Out" column of our local newspaper the other day, I came across the following:

What's In	*What's Out*
Mobile work force	Lifetime employment

So the secret is out. Now everybody knows.

I was fortunate enough to recognize that The Rules Have Changed. I used the strategies I've set down

"BIG RAISE"
STRATEGIES

▶ The tight job market will continue for years (at least until the year 2005).

▶ Many companies have no issue with Job Jumpers; in fact, they see advantages in them (fresh ideas, current market knowledge, etc.).

▶ Don't jump ship without a plan (Quit Early and Quit Often).

▶ Life is better here!

in this book and was willing and able to negotiate salary and terms. These are all things you can do, too.

What impact have they had on my life? Well, my income is through the roof. And this year my wife and I are going on a three-week vacation in northern Italy instead of touring the Oregon coast again. Hey, as they say in the commercial, *Life's better here* . . .

ABOUT THE AUTHOR

Gordon Miller has a twenty-year distinguished record in sales management positions in the Computer Services and Office Products industries. During his career he has personally coached over two hundred salespeople to win in excess of $500,000,000 in products and services contracts.

CAREER COACHING

Our purpose is to help you realize that there are significant opportunities in the U.S. job market due to the changing workplace rules, and to help you develop a career strategy to reap the financial rewards.

To help you maximize your efforts, we have created follow-up training programs for you to use—either individually or with a larger group. If you wish further information about these programs, you may contact:

The QYJO Group
P.O. Box 102335
Denver, Colorado 80250
(303) 282-9001
qyjo@rmi.net